THE 'WUNDERBAR' WORLD OF GERMAN IDIOMS VOL. 2

Discover 75 More Everyday German Idioms & Sayings

Emma Jackman

emmalovesgerman.com

Front cover design:

'Don't saw the branch you're sitting on' (page 31)

Table of Contents

Preface

Are you ready for more 'wunderbar' German idioms?

In my first book 'The Wunderbar World of German Idioms' I had decided to aim for 75 idioms as this seemed like a manageable number for both myself and my readers. After writing the first book there were quite a few idioms that didn't make it into the final version. After further research I started to uncover more and more idioms and realised I could write a second volume.

Just like in the first book, all these German idioms have been approved by German speakers as usable in everyday situations. I deliberately picked idioms that could be easily used in many situations. To keep things interesting, I've selected idioms which had English equivalents different to the German translations. Since English and German have many similarities, the two languages also share many idioms.

Each idiom has one or more examples to help you understand how to use them in context. It's not always easy to know in which situation a certain saying or idiom is suitable, but I hope these examples will help guide you.

As always when learning German, just try out a few sayings and see what reactions you get, have fun with the language and don't be afraid to try out some new sayings with friends, family and native speakers such as language exchange partners.

Free Audio Download

As a small token of thanks for buying this book, I'd like to offer a free bonus gift exclusive to my readers.

All the German idioms and example sentences are available as a free MP3 download, so you can hear the correct pronunciation as you read along in the book.

You can download the free audio here:

emmalovesgerman.com/free-audio-2

Wie Feuer und Wasser sein

Literal Translation:	To be like fire and water
Meaning:	To compare two completely different things or people
English Equivalent:	To be like chalk and cheese

Example:

Die beide Geschwister sind so unterschiedlich. Sie sind **wie Feuer und Wasser**.

The two siblings are so different. They're like chalk and cheese.

Damit lockt man keinen Hund hinter dem Ofen hervor

Literal Translation: You can't lure a dog out from behind the oven with that

Meaning: To describe something that is not very appealing or impressive

English Equivalent: It's nothing to write home about

Example:

Man kann **keinen Hund** mit der Leistung der Mannschaft **hinter dem Ofen hervorlocken**.

The team's performance is nothing to write home about.

Sich ins Knie schießen

Literal Translation:	To shoot oneself in the knee
Meaning:	To inadvertently make a situation worse
English Equivalent:	To shoot yourself in the foot

Example:

Lena hat sich über den Chef beschwert, und er kam rein und hat alles gehört! Sie hat **sich** selbst **ins Knie geschossen**.

Lena was complaining about the boss and he came in and heard everything! She really shot herself in the foot.

Note:

Another common German idiom '**sich ein Eigentor schießen**' (to shoot an own goal) has exactly the same meaning.

Ein Rad abhaben

Literal Translation: To have a wheel off

Meaning: To be a bit crazy

English Equivalent: To have a screw loose

Example:

> Ich glaube, meine neue Deutschlehrerin **hat ein Rad ab**. Sie singt vor jeder Stunde das Alphabet!

> I think my new German teacher is a bit crazy. She sings the alphabet before every lesson!

Alle Jubeljahre

Literal Translation: Every jubilee year

Meaning: To do something infrequently

English Equivalent: Once in a blue moon

Example:

Ich mache **alle Jubeljahre** Urlaub.

I have a holiday / vacation once in a blue moon.

Example:

Wenn du jeden Tag Deutsch sprichst, wirst du dich schneller verbessern, als wenn du **alle Jubeljahre** sprichst.

If you speak German everyday you'll improve faster than if you speak once in a blue moon.

Kröten schlucken

Literal Translation: To swallow toads

Meaning: To make unpalatable compromises

English Equivalent: To eat that frog

Example:

Manchmal muss man **Kröten schlucken**, um sein Ziel zu erreichen.

Sometimes you must eat that frog in order to achieve your goal.

Blaumachen

Literal Translation: To make blue

Meaning: To take a day off work or school / to skive

English Equivalent: To skip work / to throw a sickie

Example:

> Ich glaube wirklich, Maria **macht** heute **blau**.
>
> I really think Maria's skiving off today.

Example:

> Ich habe keine Urlaubstage mehr. Soll ich morgen **blaumachen**?
>
> I don't have any paid vacation days left. Should I skip work tomorrow?

Note:

> The popular 1980s US film 'Ferris Bueller's Day Off' is known in German speaking countries by its German title 'Ferris **Macht Blau**' (Ferris Makes Blue).

Den Vogel abschießen

Literal Translation: To shoot the bird off

Meaning: A very extreme behaviour

English Equivalent: That takes the cake / biscuit

Example:

Du hast schon viele verrückte Dinge in deinem Leben getan, aber das **schießt den Vogel ab**!

You've done a lot of crazy things in your life, but this takes the cake!

In vollem Gange

Literal Translation: In full progress / underway

Meaning: To describe something that is fully operational

English Equivalent: In full swing

Example:

Die Weihnachtsmärkte in Deutschland sind jetzt **in vollem Gange**.

The Christmas markets in German are now in full swing.

Ich stehe auf dich

Literal Translation: I stand on you

Meaning: To be very attracted to someone

English Equivalent: I fancy you / I have a crush on you

Example:

Um ehrlich zu sein, **ich stehe auf sie**.

To be honest, I have a crush on her.

Example:

Stehst du auf mich?

Do you fancy me?

Note:

For this phrase to be correct, we must use the accusative case (mich / dich / ihn / sie). If we use the dative case (mir / dir / ihm / ihr) the phrase means 'to stand on'.

Tomaten auf den Augen haben

Literal Translation: To have tomatoes on the eyes

Meaning: To not be aware of something obvious

English Equivalent: To be blind to something

Example:

Sie steht wirklich auf ihn, aber er **hat Tomaten auf den Augen**.

She really fancies him, but he's completely oblivious.

Ein Tropfen auf den heißen Stein

Literal Translation: A drop on the hot stone

Meaning: To describe a very small amount / effort compared to what is actually needed

English Equivalent: A drop in the ocean

Example:

Ich habe 3 Seiten meines deutschen Romans gelesen, aber das ist nur **ein Tropfen auf den heißen Stein**.

I have read 3 pages of my German novel, but it's just a drop in the ocean.

Die Wand hochgehen

Literal Translation: To go up the wall

Meaning: To be furious

English Equivalent: To go through the roof / to go up the wall

Example:

> Wenn seine Mutter das herausfindet, wird sie **die Wand hochgehen**!
>
> When his mother finds out, she'll go through the roof!

Ins Fettnäpfchen treten

Literal Translation: To step into the sand trap

Meaning: To do or say something embarrassing

English Equivalent: To put your foot in it

Example:

Sie ist erst 25 Jahre alt, aber er sagte, sie ist 40. Er ist wirklich **ins Fettnäpfchen getreten**!

She only 25 years old but he said she's 40. He really put his foot in it!

Die Tour vermasseln

Literal Translation: To mess up / screw up the tour

Meaning: To spoil someone's plans

English Equivalent: To rain on someone's parade

Example:

> Fünf Minuten vor Feierabend gibt Sandras Chef ihr noch mehr Arbeit auf. Sie hat einen schönen Abend geplant. Er hat ihre **Tour vermasselt**.

> Five minutes before the end of work, Sandra's boss gave her more work. She had a nice evening planned. He rained on her parade.

Einen Bären aufbinden

Literal Translation: To untie a bear

Meaning: To deceive someone

English Equivalent: To pull the wool over someone's eyes

Example:

Der Verkäufer lügt. Er **bindet einen Bären auf**.

The salesman is lying. He's pulling the wool over your eyes.

Sein Herz ausschüttern

Literal Translation: To pour one's heart out

Meaning: To spill your deepest feelings and emotions to someone

English Equivalent: To pour your heart out

Example:

Nach der Auflösung meiner Ehr, habe ich einer Freundin **mein Herz ausgeschüttert**.

After the breakdown of my marriage, I poured my heart out to a friend.

Das ist mir Wurst

Literal Translation: That is sausage to me

Meaning: To express indifference

English Equivalent: It doesn't bother me / I don't care

Example:

    - Was wollen wir heute Abend?
    - **Das ist mir Wurst**.

    - What shall we do this evening?
    - I don't mind.

Auf hundertachtzig bringen

Literal Translation: To bring at 180

Meaning: To get really angry / wound up

English Equivalent: To be hopping mad

Example:

> Wenn ich die Nachrichten gucke, **bringe** ich mich oft **auf hundertachtzig**.

> When I watch the news, I often get really angry.

Übers Ohr hauen

Literal Translation: To bash over the ears

Meaning: To con / deceive someone

English Equivalent: To pull a fast one / to stitch up

Example:

Ich habe dieses Auto letzte Woche gekauft und jetzt ist es kaputt. Ich glaube, sie haben mich **übers Ohr gehauen**.

I bought this car last week, and now it's broken. I think they've stitched me up.

Ein Glückspilz sein

Literal Translation: To be a lucky mushroom

Meaning: To describe someone who is very lucky

English Equivalent: To be a lucky devil

Example:

Mein Nachbar hat im Lotto gewonnen, was für **ein Glückspilz**!

My neighbour won the lottery, what a lucky devil!

Geld auf den Kopf hauen

Literal Translation: To hit / put money on the head

Meaning: To spend money freely and without care

English Equivalent: To throw money around

Example:

Seitdem mein Nachbar im Lotto gewonnen hat, hat er das **Geld auf den Kopf gehauen**. Er hat mir sogar 100€ gegeben!

Since my neighbour won the lottery, he's thrown money around. He even gave me 100 Euros!

Einen grünen Daumen haben

Literal Translation:	To have a green thumb
Meaning:	To be a keen gardener
English Equivalent:	To have green fingers

Example:

Meine Eltern lieben es, im Garten zu arbeiten. Sie **haben einen grünen Daumen**.

My parents love to work in the garden. They have green fingers.

Seinen Senf dazugeben

Literal Translation: To give their mustard

Meaning: To give an opinion

English Equivalent: To put their two cents in

Example:

Ich weiß, was ich in meinem Leben will, aber Papa **gibt** trotzdem immer **seinen Senf dazu**.

I know what I want in my life, but Dad still always puts in his two cents.

Man soll den Tag nicht vor dem Abend loben

Literal Translation: One should not praise the day before the evening

Meaning: To not celebrate prematurely

English Equivalent: Don't count your chickens before they've hatched

Example:

> - Ich denke, ich habe mich beim Vorstellungsgespräch wirklich gut geschlagen.
>
> - Ja sicher, aber **man soll den Tag nicht vor Abend loben**.

> - I think I did really well at my interview.
>
> - Yes sure, but you shouldn't count your chickens before they've hatched.

So flach wie ein Brett

Literal Translation: As flat as a board

Meaning: To describe something that is very flat

English Equivalent: As flat as a pancake

Example:

> Er hat den Ball mit dem Auto umgefahren. Er ist jetzt **so flach wie ein Brett**.

> He ran over the ball with the car. Now it's as flat as a pancake.

Bei jemand einen Stein im Brett haben

Literal Translation: To have a stone on the board with someone

Meaning: To have won favour with someone

English Equivalent: To be in someone's good books

Example:

Ich habe meinem Freund beim Umzug geholfen, also habe ich **bei ihm einen Stein im Brett**.

I helped my friend move house, so I'm in his good books.

Die Beine in die Hand nehmen

Literal Translation: To take the legs in the hand

Meaning: To run away very fast

English Equivalent: To make a quick getaway

Example:

Die Bankräuber hatte **die Beine in die Hand genommen**.

The bank robber made a quick getaway.

Säge nicht am Ast, auf dem du sitzt

Literal Translation: Don't saw the branch you're sitting on

Meaning: Don't be unkind to someone who helps you

English Equivalent: Don't bite the hand that feeds you

Example:

Wenn sie Hilfe braucht, sollte sie **nicht am Ast sägen, auf dem sie sitzt**.

If she needs help, she shouldn't bite the hand that feeds her.

Etwas auf dem Herzen haben

Literal Translation: To have something on the heart

Meaning: To have a lot to think about, possibly distracted

English Equivalent: To have something on one's mind

Example:

Eine Freundin **hat** im Moment **viel auf dem Herzen**.

A friend has a lot on her mind at the moment.

Example:

Wenn du **etwas auf dem Herzen hast**, kannst du es mir einfach sagen.

If you have something on your mind, you can just tell me.

Im Schneckentempo

Literal Translation: At the snail speed

Meaning: To describe something extremely slow

English Equivalent: At a snail's pace

Example:

Der heutige Tag verläuft **im Schneckentempo**.

Today is going at a snail's pace.

Etwas hinter die Ohren schreiben

Literal Translation: To write something behind the ears

Meaning: To make a note of something / to not forget something

English Equivalent: To make a mental note

Example:

- Vergiss nicht, heute deinen Reisepass abzuholen.

- Ich **schreibe es mir hinter die Ohren**.

- Don't forget to pick up your passport today.

- I'll make a mental note.

Kein Zuckerschlecken

Literal Translation: No sugar lick

Meaning: To describe something that is not easy to achieve

English Equivalent: No walk in the park

Example:

Die deutsche B2-Prüfung ist **kein Zuckerschlecken.**

The German B2 exam is no walk in the park.

Ein Schuss in den Ofen

Literal Translation: A shot into the oven

Meaning: To fail at something

English Equivalent: To fail miserably

Example:

Mein Versuch, das Auto zu reparieren, war **ein Schuss in den Ofen**.

My attempt to fix the car failed miserably.

08/15 (Nullachtfünfzehn)

Literal Translation: Zero eight fifteen

Meaning: To describe something that is average / mediocre

English Equivalent: Run of the mill

Example:

Um ehrlich zu sein, war die ganze Show **nullachtfünfzehn**.

To be honest, the whole show was fairly run of the mill.

Note:

In the German version of Disney's The Little Mermaid, Ursula explains to Ariel what she must do to remain a human forever:

Keinen **08/15** Kuss, nur der Kuss der wahren Liebe.

Not just any kiss, only the kiss of true love.

Einen Hals haben

Literal Translation: To have a neck

Meaning: To be angry / disappointed

English Equivalent: To be hopping mad

Example:

Ich **habe** so **einen Hals** auf dich!

I'm so angry with you!

Example:

Ich konnte nicht glauben, dass das Auto im Urlaub eine Panne hatte.
Ich **hatte** so **einen Hals**.

I couldn't believe that car broke down on holiday. I was so angry.

Wasser predigen und Wein trinken

Literal Translation: To preach water and drink wine

Meaning: To be a hypocrite / to not behave in the way you tell others to behave

English Equivalent: To not practice what you preach

Example:

> Monika sagt ihren Kindern, sie sollen nicht zu viel fernsehen, aber sie sieht selbst zu viel fern. Sie **predigt Wasser und trinkt Wein**.

> Monika tells her children not to watch too much TV, but she watches too much TV herself. She doesn't practice what she preaches.

Das Licht der Welt erblicken

Literal Translation: To see the light of the world

Meaning: To be born / to begin to exist or become available to the public

English Equivalent: To see the light of day

Example:

Mit etwas Glück wird dieses schreckliche Projekt nie **das Licht der Welt erblicken**.

With a bit of luck this dreadful project will never see the light of day.

Example:

Das Baby **erblickte** vor wenigen Stunden **das Licht der Welt**.

The baby was born a few hours ago.

Halt die Ohren steif

Literal Translation: Keep the ears stiff

Meaning: Used to encourage someone to remain positive in a bad situation

English Equivalent: Keep your chin up

Example:

Ich weiß, dass du deinen Job verloren hast, aber du wirst einen neuen finden. **Halt die Ohren steif**.

I know that you lost your job, but you'll find another one. Keep your chin up.

Mit den Wolfen heulen

Literal Translation: To howl with the wolves

Meaning: To conform (often negative)

English Equivalent: To go along with the crowd / to follow the herd

Example:

Anstatt ihren eigenen Weg zu gehen, **heult** sie **mit den Wölfen**.

Instead of following her own path, she's going along with the crowd.

Das Herz auf der Zunge tragen

Literal Translation: To wear the heart on the tongue

Meaning: To show one's feelings openly

English Equivalent: To wear your heart on your sleeve

Example:

Ich trage **mein Herz auf der Zunge** und erzähle Bekannte oft zu viel über mein Privatleben.

I wear my heart on my sleeve and often tell acquaintances too much about my private life.

Einen Vogel haben

Literal Translation: To have a bird

Meaning: To be crazy

English Equivalent: To go nuts

Example:

> Jonas verkaufte sein gesamtes Hab und Gut und machte eine Rucksacktour durch Südamerika. Er **hat einen Vogel**!

> Jonas sold all his belongings and went backpacking across south America. He's nuts!

Das ist nicht mein Bier

Literal Translation: That's not my beer

Meaning: Used for something that is private information

English Equivalent: That's none of my business

Example:

- Was hältst du davon, dass Jonas seinen Job kündigt und mit dem Rucksack durch Südamerika reist?

- **Das ist nicht mein Bier**.

- What do you think about Jonas quitting his job and backpacking across South America?

- It's none of my business.

An den Rand der Verzweiflung bringen

Literal Translation: To bring to the edge of despair

Meaning: To describe someone who has lost all hope

English Equivalent: On the brink

Example:

So viel Pech hat mich **an den Rand Verzweiflung gebracht**.

So much bad luck has brought me to the brink of despair.

Einen klaren Kopf behalten

Literal Translation: To keep a clear head

Meaning: To describe being able to think clearly especially in difficult situations

English Equivalent: To keep a clear head

Example:

In eine Krise schaffe ich es, **einen klaren Kopf zu behalten**.

In a crisis I manage to keep a clear head.

Seine Brötchen verdienen

Literal Translation:	To earn the bread rolls
Meaning:	To describe how someone earns money
English Equivalent:	To bring home the bacon / to make a living

Example:

Ich **verdiene meine Brötchen** mit einem Nebenjob.

I make a living with a part-time job.

Das kannst du deiner Oma erzählen

Literal Translation: You can tell that to your grandmother

Meaning: To express disbelief (often used sarcastically)

English Equivalent: Yeah right! / I don't believe a word of it!

Example:

- Ich laufe nächste Woche einen Marathon.
- **Das kannst du deiner Oma erzählen**!

- I'm running a marathon next week.
- Yeah right!

Die Zeit vergeht wie im Flug

Literal Translation: Time goes like in flight

Meaning: To describe how time moves along quickly

English Equivalent: Time flies

Example:

Die Zeit vergeht wie im Flug, wenn man Spaß macht.

Time flies when you're having fun.

An den Haaren herbeigezogen

Literal Translation: To be dragged along by the hair

Meaning: To be very unlikely / unbelievable

English Equivalent: To be far-fetched

Example:

Die Geschichte mit dem Drachen und den fliegenden Autos **ist an den Haaren herbeigezogen**.

The story with the dragon and the flying cars is far-fetched.

Im siebten Himmel sein

Literal Translation: To be in seventh heaven

Meaning: To be completely happy / content

English Equivalent: To be in seventh heaven / on cloud nine

Example:

In den ersten Monaten meiner neuen Beziehung **war ich im siebten Himmel**.

For the first few months of my new relationship, I was on cloud nine.

Auf der anderen Seite ist das Gras viel grüner

Literal Translation: On the other side the grass is much greener

Meaning: The belief that other people have it better than you

English Equivalent: The grass is always greener on the other side

Example:

Sie will ihren Job kündigen und YouTuberin werden. Sie glaubt, **das Gras ist auf der anderen Seite viel grüner.**

She want to quit her job and become a YouTuber. She believes the grass is greener on the other side.

Example:

Das Gras auf der anderen Seite ist nicht immer **grüner.**

The grass isn't always greener on the other side.

Zum Sankt Nimmerleinstag

Literal Translation: On Saint Nimmerlein's Day

Meaning: To describe an activity that is unproductive or futile

English Equivalent: Until the cows come home

Example:

Wir können bis **zum Sankt Nimmerleinstag** darüber reden, aber ich werde nie nach Hause zurückkehren.

We can talk about it until the cows come home, but I'm never going back home.

Das Handtuch werfen

Literal Translation: To throw the towel

Meaning: To give up / to quit

English Equivalent: To throw in the towel

Example:

> Wenn man ein neues Unternehmen gründet, ist das leicht entmutigt zu werden und **das Handtuch werfen**.

> When you start a new business it's easy to become discouraged and throw in the towel.

Am Ball bleiben

Literal Translation: To stay on the ball

Meaning: To not become overwhelmed

English Equivalent: To stay on the ball / to stay on top of things

Example:

Wenn auf der Arbeit viel los ist, ist es wichtig, **am Ball zu bleiben**.

When there's a lot going on at work, it's important to stay on the ball.

Kein Blatt vor den Mund nehmen

Literal Translation: To take no sheet in front of the mouth

Meaning: To describe someone who is very direct

English Equivalent: To not mince one's words

Example:

Maria ist typisch deutsch und ziemlich direkt. **Sie nimmt kein Blatt vor den Mund**.

Maria is stereotypically German and quite direct. She doesn't mince her words.

Geld aus dem Fenster werfen

Literal Translation: To throw money out of the window

Meaning: To waste money

English Equivalent: To pour money down the drain

Example:

Diese Regierung **wirft das Geld** einfach **aus dem Fenster**.

This government just pours money down the drain.

Ein Spatz in der Hand ist besser als eine Taube auf dem Dach

Literal Translation: A sparrow in the hand is better than a pigeon on the roof

Meaning: It's better to hold onto something you already have, than risk losing everything pursuing something better

English Equivalent: A bird in the hand is better than two in the bush

Example:

Wenn Sie Ihren Job nicht mögen, sollten Sie nicht kündigen, bevor Sie einen neuen haben. **Ein Spatz in der Hand ist besser als eine Taube auf dem Dach**.

If you don't like your job, you shouldn't quit before you have a new one. A bird in the hand is better than two in the bush.

Tote Hose

Literal Translation: Dead trousers

Meaning: Something is boring or nothing is happening

English Equivalent: It's dead

Example:

Wir sind in einem kleinen Dorf in Frankreich übernachtet. Das ist **tote Hose**.

We stayed in a small village in France. It's totally dead there.

Vor Neid platzen

Literal Translation: To burst from envy

Meaning: To be extremely envious

English Equivalent: To be green with envy

Example:

Wenn ich meiner Freundin erzählt, dass ich Brad Pitt getroffen habe, wird sie **vor Neid platzen**!

When I tell my friend that I met Brad Pitt, she'll be green with envy!

Die Beine / Füße hochlegen

Literal Translation: To put the legs / feet up

Meaning: To relax / not overexert oneself

English Equivalent: To put your feet up

Example:

> Das Beste, was man tun kann, wenn man krank ist, ist **die Beine hochzulegen**.
>
> The best thing you can do when you're sick, is to put your feet up.

Wieder auf den Beinen / Füße

Literal Translation: On the legs / feet again

Meaning: To recover after a negative experience or event

English Equivalent: To get back on your feet

Example:

Er war ziemlich krank, aber jetzt ist er **wieder auf den Beinen**.

He was quite ill, but he's now back on his feet again.

Die Kirche im Dorf lassen

Literal Translation:	To leave the church in the village
Meaning:	To not get overexcited
English Equivalent:	To not get carried away / To not go overboard

Example:

> Es ist toll, dass du eine Gehaltserhöhung bekommen hast, aber **lass die Kirche im Dorf** und gibt nicht alles aus.

> It's great that you got a pay rise, but don't get carried away and spend it all.

(In der) Luftlinie

Literal Translation: In the air line

Meaning: To measure the distance between two points in a straight line

English Equivalent: As the crow flies

Example:

Bremen und Hamburg sind 98km **Luftlinie** voreinander entfernt.

Bremen and Hamburg are 98km apart as the crow flies.

Gibt man ihm den kleinen Finger, nimmt er die ganze Hand

Literal Translation: To give someone the little finger, they take the whole hand

Meaning: To describe someone who takes advantage of someone's generosity

English Equivalent: To give someone an inch and they take a mile

Example:

Ich habe meinem Bruder mein Auto geliehen und er ist nach Italien gefahren! **Gibt man ihm den kleinen Finger, nimmt er die ganze Hand.**

I lent my car to my brother and he drove to Italy! Give someone an inch and they take a mile.

Die Kuh vom Eis holen

Literal Translation: To get the cow off the ice

Meaning: To try to solve a difficult situation

English Equivalent: To rescue the situation / to avoid a disaster

Example:

Um **die Kuh vom Eis zu holen**, müssen wir die ganze Nacht an diesem Projekt arbeiten.

In order to avoid a disaster, we have to work on this project all night.

Gas geben

Literal Translation: To give gas

Meaning: To encourage someone to hurry / to urge someone to drive faster

English Equivalent: To put your foot down / to step on it

Example:

Wir müssen **Gas geben**, um diese Arbeit rechtzeitig zu erledigen.

We need to step on it to get this work done on time.

Example:

Los, **gib Gas**, wir werden zu spät kommen!

Go, step on it, we're going to be late!

Die beleidigte Leberwurst spielen

Literal Translation: To play the offended liver sausage

Meaning: To describe someone who is sulking

English Equivalent: To be in a huff

Example:

Ich habe meinen Bruder beim Tennis geschlagen und jetzt **spielt er die beleidigende Leberwurst**.

I beat my brother at tennis and now he's in a huff.

Ein Fisch auf dem Trockenen

Literal Translation: A fish on the dry

Meaning: To describe someone who is out of their normal environment

English Equivalent: A fish out of water

Example:

Als ich das erste Mal allein nach Deutschland kam, fühlte ich mich wie **ein Fisch auf dem Trockenen**.

The first time I went to Germany alone, I felt like a fish out of water.

Ich glaube, mein Schwein pfeift

Literal Translation: I believe my pig is whistling

Meaning: To express disbelief

English Equivalent: I don't believe it / You've got to be kidding me

Example:

- Ich habe gehört, dass der Chef gesagt hat, er würde uns eine Lohnerhöhung geben.

- **Ich glaube, mein Schwein pfeift!**

- I heard the boss say that he'd give us a pay rise.

- You've got to be kidding me!

Das fünfte Rad am Wagen sein

Literal Translation: To be the fifth wheel on the car

Meaning: To describe someone who is not wanted or welcome in a group

English Equivalent: To be a third wheel

Example:

Es ist nett von euch, dass ihr mich zu eurem Date einladet, aber ich möchte nicht **das fünfte Rad am Wagen sein.**

It's nice of you guys to invite me to your date, but I don't want to be a third wheel.

Eine Extrawurst verlangen / bekommen

Literal Translation: To demand / get an extra sausage

Meaning: To describe someone who always wants something special

English Equivalent: To demand / get special treatment

Example:

Lena **verlangt** immer **eine Extrawurst**. Sie wollte ein kostenloses Flug-Upgrade.

Lena always demands special treatment. She wanted a free flight upgrade.

Da kannst du Gift darauf nehmen

Literal Translation: You can take poison on it

Meaning: Used for saying something is certain or almost guaranteed

English Equivalent: You can bet your life on it / You betcha!

Example:

    - Wird Lukas mit uns nach Spanien kommen?
    - **Da kannst du Gift darauf nehmen**!

    - Will Luka come with us to Spain?
    - You betcha!

Jetzt haben wir den Salat

Literal Translation: Now we have the salad

Meaning: To describe a situation that has gone wrong despite prior warnings

English Equivalent: Now we've had it / Now we're in a pickle

Example:

Ich habe dir gesagt, du sollst den Knopf nicht drücken, **jetzt haben wir den Salat!**

I told you not to press that button, now we've had it!

Alles in Butter

Literal Translation:	Everything in butter
Meaning:	Used to indicate that everything is ok
English Equivalent:	Everything's hunky dory

Example:

Ich hätte fast meinen Flug verpasst, aber jetzt ist **alles in Butter**.

I almost missed my flight, but now everything's ok.

Das Gelbe vom Ei sein

Literal Translation: To be the yellow of the egg

Meaning: To describe something favourably

English Equivalent: The best thing since sliced bread / the bees knees

Opposite: Nothing to write home about

Example:

Von allen deutschen Städten ist Bremen meiner Meinung nach **das Gelbe vom Ei**.

Of all the German cities, in my opinion Bremen is the best.

Example:

Der neueste Superheldenfilm war **nicht** gerade **das Gelbe vom Ei**.

That latest superhero film was nothing to write home about.

What did you think of this book?

First of all, thank you for purchasing 'The Wunderbar World of German Idioms Vol. 2'. I know you could have picked any number of books to read, but you picked this book and for that I am extremely grateful.

I hope that it helped you to understand more about German idioms. If you found this book helpful, it would be great if you could share this book with your friends and family by posting to Facebook and Twitter.

If you enjoyed this book and found some benefit in reading this, I'd like to hear from you and hope that you could take some time to post a review on Amazon. Your feedback and support will help me to greatly improve my writing craft for future projects and make this book even better.

About the Author

Emma Jackman is the founder of EmmaLovesGerman.com. She started learning German as an adult at the age of 34 after many years visiting Germany but being unable to speak the language.

She is dedicated to helping others learn to love the German language as much as she does, and to make this sometimes confusing language, that bit easier.

EmmaLovesGerman.com is an all-round resource for German learners. There you'll find articles about speaking, reading, listening and writing in German as well as simplifying German grammar, explaining frequently used phrases and reviewing online language courses and resources.

Printed in Great Britain
by Amazon

84463360R00051